G000152064

CAKETAILS

OVER 18

INTOXICATING CUPCAKES FOR GROWN UPS

First published in 2013 by Chef Books.

Chef Books
Network House, 28 Ballmoor, Celtic Court
Buckingham MK18 1RQ, UK
www.chefmagazine.co.uk

ISBN 978-1-908202-16-1

Printed by C.T. Printing in China

AUTHORS: JILL COLLINS AND NATALIE SAVILLE

PUBLISHER: PETER MARSHALL

MANAGING EDITOR: SHIRLEY MARSHALL

SUB EDITOR: HELEN HOMES

PHOTOGRAPHER: PETER MARSHALL

DESIGNER: PHILIP DONNELLY

When we first heard about caketails a year or so ago, we though they sounded great fun and wanted to try them out for ourselves. However – as with everything we bake – we wanted to make sure that our caketails would taste as good as they look.

Our two previous books ('Cake Decorating with the Kids', and 'Bake Me I'm Yours.... Whoopie Pies'), had majored in decorating rather than baking techniques, so for us, it was an opportunity to go back to basics and really experiment with flavours and ideas to create a completely new set of recipes.

And after all, what could be more fun than sampling all the original cocktails, and then trying to replicate them in a cupcake? Diets went out of the window as we chopped, caramelised, soaked and baked. We had numerous days when we would dream up recipes and then put them together in a finished product for our families and friends to try (our children were particularly annoyed that they couldn't have a nibble, but after all – if you're going to have alcohol in a cupcake, you might as well be able to taste it!!)

The challenge came with trying to ensure that each recipe had an explosion of flavours which really did reflect all aspects of the original cocktails. We achieved this not only by flavouring both the cupcakes and the buttercreams with the main alcoholic drinks represented in the original cocktails, but also by adding the relevant fruits to the mix where feasible – usually pre-soaked decadently in alcohol.

But being us, we couldn't resist throwing in some decorating options too, so you will find that for each caketail, we have suggested three ways of decorating, based on how much time (or inclination) you have, or the occasion you are making them for. So whether you're planning an intimate Valentine's evening for two, or a Black Tie event for 100, you will find a selection of deliciously intoxicating caketail recipes to try. And needless to say – however you decide to decorate them – you can be assured they will all taste amazing.

Happy baking!

JILL & NATALIE
THE GREAT LITTLE CAKE COMPANY

VALENTINES

NAUGHTY BUT NICE

BLACK TIE

COCKTAILS

SUMMER

HALLOWEEN

CHRISTMAS

TIPS AND TECHNIQUES

PREPARATION AND PLANNING:

It is always important to read each recipe through to the end well in advance of baking, as some of our recipes involve pre-soaking fruit in alcohol, or pre-baking decorations.

Cupcakes are always best eaten on the day they are baked, but if you are busy they can be made a couple of weeks in advance, frozen in airtight containers and thawed for a couple of hours before you need them.

Meringues can also be made a couple of days in advance and stored in a cool dry place to retain crispness

Buttercream can be made in advance too, and stored in the fridge for a week or two, or the freezer for up to a month. Just remove a couple of hours before needed and allow to return to room temperature. If its too stiff to pipe, a few seconds in the microwave does the trick.

Fresh cream toppings are best made just before use and eaten immediately.

BAKING:

All our recipes are for 12 cupcakes. We use large cupcake cases, so if you use smaller ones, you will be able to make more cupcakes.
All eggs are medium unless otherwise specified (we use free range).
All spoon measurements are level.
All cooking times are approximate as all ovens vary, and cupcake cases come in many different sizes.

FOOD COLOURING:

If at all possible, use paste rather than liquid food colouring, as it has less effect on the balance of the recipe. If you only have liquid colour, just reduce the amount of alcohol slightly to compensate.

GLITTERING:

Moisten the item with a barely damp paintbrush and sprinkle liberally with glitter. Place a piece of paper underneath to collect any excess for re-use.

CAKETAILS

CONVERSION CHART
WEIGHT (SOLIDS)

¼oz	5g
½oz	10g
¾oz	20g
1oz	25g
1 ½oz	40g
2oz	50g
2 ½oz	60g
¾oz	75g
4oz	110g
4 ½oz	125g
5 ½oz	150g
6oz	175g
7oz (2 cups)	200g
8oz (½lb)	225g
9oz	250g
10oz	275g
10 ½oz (3 cups)	300g
12oz (¾lb)	350g
13oz	375g
14oz (4 cups)	400g
1lb	450g
1lb 8oz	700g (1/2 kg)
2lb	900g
3lb	1.35kg
3lb 5oz	1.5kg
4lb	1.8kg

VOLUME (LIQUIDS)

1 teaspoon (tsp)	5ml
1 dessertspoon	10ml
1 tablespoon (tbsp)	15ml or ½fl oz
1 fl oz	30ml
1 ½ fl oz	40ml
2 fl oz	60ml
3 fl oz	75ml
3 ½ fl oz	100ml
4 fl oz	120ml
5 fl oz	150ml or ¼ pint (pt)
6 fl oz	175ml
7 fl oz	200ml
8 fl oz	240ml
9 fl oz	260ml
10 fl oz	275ml or ½ pint
11 fl oz	325ml
12 fl oz	350ml
13 fl oz	375ml
14 fl oz	400ml
15 fl oz	450ml or ¾ pint
16 fl oz	475ml
18 fl oz	500ml (½ litre)
19 fl oz	550ml
20 fl oz	600ml or 1 pint
1 ¼ pints	725ml
1 ½ pints	875ml
1 ¾ pints	1 litre
2 pints	1.2 litres
2 ½ pints	1.5 litres
3 pints	1.7 litres
3 ½ pints	2 litres
1 qt	950ml
2 qt	1 litre
3 qt	2.25 litres
4 qt	4.5 litres
5 qt	5.5 litres

LENGTH

¼ inch (")	5mm
½ inch	1cm
¾ inch	2cm
1 inch	2 ½cm
1 ¼ inches	3cm
1 ½ inches	4cm
2 inches	5cm
3 inches	7 ½cm
4 inches	10cm
6 inches	15cm
7 inches	18cm
8 inches	20cm
10 inches	25 ½cm
11 inches	28cm
12 inches	30cm

OVEN TEMPERATURES

Celsius*	Fahrenheit	Gas	Description
110°C	225°F	Gas Mark	¼ Cool
120°C	250°F	Gas Mark	½ Cool
140°C	275°F	Gas Mark 1	Very low
150°C	300°F	Gas Mark 2	Very low
170°C	325°F	Gas Mark 3	Low
180°C	350°F	Gas Mark 4	Moderate
190°C	375°F	Gas Mark 5	Moderate, Hot
200°C	400°F	Gas Mark 6	Hot
220°C	425°F	Gas Mark 7	Hot
230°C	450°F	Gas Mark 8	Very hot
240°C	475°F	Gas Mark 9	Very hot

* For fan assisted ovens, reduce temperatures by 20°C

TEMPERATURE CONVERSION: 0°C = 32°F

PS I LOVE YOU

ITS ALWAYS GOOD TO HAVE LOVE TO KEEP YOU WARM — AND THIS EXQUISITE CAKETAIL, TOPPED WITH RICH DARK CHOCOLATE AND SMOOTH BAILEY'S CREAM, IS A CUDDLE IN A CUPCAKE!

preparation time:
20 minutes

cooking time:
24 minutes

Makes 12 cupcakes

ℹ

Cupcakes:
165g unsalted butter (softened)
165g caster sugar
3 medium eggs
165g self raising flour (sifted)
50ml Amaretto liqueur
1 heaped tsp espresso powder
3-4 tbsp Kahlua for drizzling

Baileys buttercream:
250g unsalted butter (softened)
500g icing sugar
100ml Baileys Irish cream
  liqueur
Piping bag with large round or
  star nozzle

Baileys cream:
600ml double cream
4 tbsp Baileys Irish cream
  liqueur
2 tbsp icing sugar
Piping bag with large round or
  star nozzle

m

1. Preheat the oven to 180°C (160°C fan).
2. Cream the butter and sugar until light and fluffy.
3. Add the eggs one at a time, beating well in-between each egg to avoid curdling.
4. Dissolve the espresso powder in the Amaretto liqueur. Beat in one third of the flour, followed by half the liqueur mixture, and beat until fully incorporated. Repeat, finishing with the remaining flour.
5. Fill the cupcake cases two thirds full and bake in the centre of the oven for 24 minutes, or until a skewer inserted in the middle of a cupcake comes out clean.
6. Once cooked, allow the cakes to cool in the tin for 5 minutes, then remove and continue to cool on a wire rack.
7. Once cool, make holes in the top of each cupcake using a skewer, and drizzle generously with Kahlua for a lovely rich coffee hit.

Baileys buttercream:

1. Beat the butter with an electric whisk until light and fluffy. Sieve the icing sugar into the butter, add the Baileys and fold together using a flat knife.
2. Once most of the icing sugar has been incorporated, finish beating with the whisk to make a lovely rich buttercream.

Baileys cream:

Whip the cream, Baileys and icing sugar together until soft peaks form. This is best eaten immediately.

PS I LOVE YOU

1 CREAMY COFFEE

Espresso powder

Using a large star nozzle,
pipe a swirl of Baileys
buttercream onto each
cupcake and sprinkle
with espresso powder.

2 CONFETTI & CHOCOLATE

Dark chocolate (approx 50g)
Mini heart sprinkles
Small piping bag

To make the chocolate shapes, melt the chocolate in a microwave or bain marie, and spoon into a small piping bag. Snip off the tip, and then indulge your creative side by piping an assortment of hearts, swirls, spirals – or even your loved one's initials – onto a baking tray lined with non-stick baking parchment. Pop into the fridge for 15-20 minutes or so until set, then peel off carefully and rest on the buttercream swirl. Pipe a swirl of Baileys buttercream onto each cupcake, scatter with mini heart sprinkles and top with a chocolate squiggle or heart.

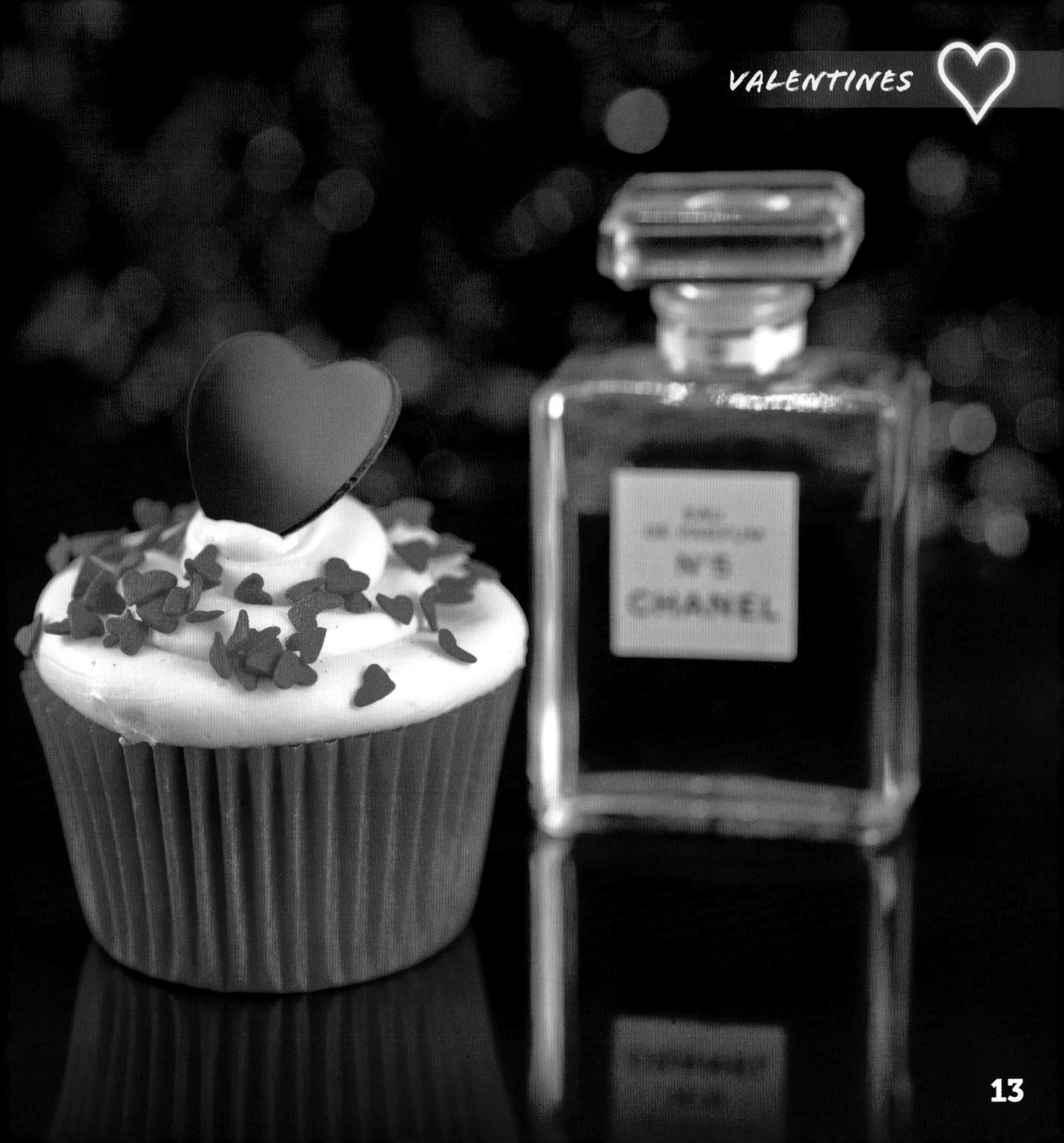
N°5
CHANEL

PS I LOVE YOU

3 RICH & DARK

Cocktail glasses
Kahlua or chocolate sauce to taste
Maraschino cherries

This cupcake looks deliciously decadent presented
in a cocktail glass. First, cut each cupcake in half
horizontally, then pipe a swirl of Baileys cream at
the bottom of each glass. Top with a round of cake,
then repeat, finishing with a swirl of cream on top.
If you fancy a really rich treat, drizzle some Kahlua
or chocolate sauce on top. Decorate with a chocolate
decoration (see p12) and a maraschino cherry –
the perfect deconstructed cupcake!

STRAWBERRY DAIQUIRI

SOFT JUICY STRAWBERRIES AND WARMING AROMATIC RUM ARE A PERFECT COMBINATION FOR VALENTINES DAY. GO ON – INDULGE YOURSELVES!

preparation time:
25 minutes excluding soaking time

cooking time:
24 minutes

Makes 12 cupcakes

i

Cupcakes:
165g unsalted butter (softened)
165g caster sugar
3 medium eggs
220g self raising flour (sifted)
5 chopped strawberries (approx 100g)
30ml white rum
3-4 tbsp extra rum for drizzling

Strawberry buttercream:
250g unsalted butter (softened)
500g icing sugar
60ml white rum
3 large strawberries (finely chopped, otherwise, they won't pass through the nozzle)
Piping bag with large round nozzle

m

1. Place the chopped strawberries and rum into a container to soak and set aside to macerate for a few minutes or up to an hour, stirring occasionally, to allow the flavours to infuse and develop. Don't leave for more than an hour as the strawberries will lose their vibrant colour and go too soft.
2. Preheat the oven to 180°C (160°C fan).
3. Cream the butter and sugar until light and fluffy.
4. Add the eggs one at a time, beating well in-between each egg to avoid curdling. Beat in one third of the flour, followed by half the strawberry/rum mixture, and beat until fully incorporated. Repeat , finishing with the remaining flour.
5. Fill the cupcake cases two thirds full and bake in the centre of the oven for 24 minutes, or until a skewer inserted in the middle of a cupcake comes out clean.
6. Once cooked, allow the cakes to cool in the tin for 5 minutes, then remove and continue to cool completely on a wire rack. Once cooled, make holes in the top of each cupcake using a skewer, and drizzle generously with rum.

Strawberry buttercream:
1. Beat the butter with an electric whisk until light and fluffy. Sieve the icing sugar into the butter, add the rum and fold together using a flat knife.
2. Once most of the icing sugar has been incorporated, finish beating with the whisk to combine fully, and then gently fold in the chopped strawberries to finish – not too much, as you want to retain the lovely jewelled look of the individual pieces of fruit.

STRAWBERRY DAIQUIRI

1 STRAWBERRY SYRUP

Grated lime zest
Strawberry syrup

Using a large round nozzle, pipe a swirl of strawberry buttercream onto each cupcake, grate lime zest over the tops and drizzle with strawberry syrup. You could always mix the syrup with a little rum for an extra kick.

STRAWBERRY DAIQUIRI

2 DOUBLE STRAWBERRY

Freeze dried strawberries
Fresh strawberries

Pipe a swirl of strawberry buttercream onto each
cupcake using a large round nozzle, then roll the edge
of each cupcake in freeze dried strawberries to create a
decorated rim.
Top with a fresh strawberry for a mouthful of summer.

STRAWBERRY DAIQUIRI

3 MARVELLOUS MERINGUES

4 large eggs whites
250g caster sugar
2 tsp cornflour
½ tsp vanilla extract
1 tsp white vinegar
6g freeze dried strawberries

1 tsp strawberry syrup
Red paste food colouring
Lime zest
large piping bag
large round nozzle

MAKE THESE A DOUBLE TREAT BY TOPPING EACH CAKETAIL WITH A DELICIOUSLY GOOEY STRAWBERRY MERINGUE.

MERINGUES

1. Preheat the oven to 180°C (160°C fan).
2. Beat the egg whites until foamy, then add the sugar (1 tablespoon at a time) and beat until white and glossy. Add the cornflour, vanilla extract, vinegar and strawberry syrup and fold in gently to combine. Add the freeze dried strawberries and a touch of pink paste food colouring to the meringue and gently fold in, leaving streaks of the colour unmixed, to give a lovely marbled effect.
3. Draw twelve circles (approx 8cms, depending on the size of your cupcake) onto a piece of non stick baking parchment and turn this upside down on a baking tray. Pile the meringue mixture into a large piping bag fitted with a large round nozzle and pipe meringue swirls inside each circle.
   The meringue doesn't spread much, so you can pipe right to the edge.
4. Lower the oven temperature to 155°C (135°C fan), pop the baking tray into the centre of the oven, and bake for 30 minutes. Turn off the oven, then leave the meringues inside to cool for a further 30 minutes.

Once the meringues have cooled, pipe a swirl of strawberry buttercream onto each cupcake, and top with a meringue. Sprinkle with grated lime zest and a few extra freeze dried strawberries.

BELLINI

CHAMPAGNE IS OUR FIRST THOUGHT WHATEVER THE CELEBRATION — BUT ESPECIALLY ON VALENTINE'S DAY. AND THERE'S SOMETHING PARTICULARLY ROMANTIC ABOUT A BELLINI — WITH ITS SWEET AROMATIC PEACHINESS AND SPARKLING MOUSSE.

preparation time:
35 minutes excluding soaking time

cooking time:
24 minutes

Makes 12 cupcakes

i

Cupcakes:
165g unsalted butter (softened)
165g caster sugar
3 medium eggs
165g self raising flour (sifted)
25ml peach purée
25ml peach schnapps

And to fill:
2 ripe peaches very finely chopped although you can leave the skins on
2 tbsp peach schnapps
Apple corer

Champagne buttercream:
250g unsalted butter (softened)
500g icing sugar
125ml champagne/sparkling wine
Peach food colouring (optional)
Piping bag with large round or star nozzle

m

1. To make the filling: place the chopped peaches and peach schnapps into a container to soak, cover with clingfilm and leave for an hour or so, stirring occasionally. Try not to leave them too long, as the peaches tend to turn brown, and don't look as fresh and vibrant as they should.
2. Preheat the oven to 180ºC (160ºC fan).
3. Cream the butter and sugar until light and fluffy.
4. Add the eggs one at a time, beating well in-between each egg to avoid curdling. Beat in one third of the flour, followed by half the peach purée/schnapps mixture, and beat until fully incorporated. Repeat, finishing with the remaining flour.
5. Fill the cupcake cases two thirds full and bake in the centre of the oven for 24 minutes, or until a skewer inserted in the middle of a cupcake comes out clean.
6. Once cooked, allow the cakes to cool in the tin for 5 minutes, then remove and cool completely on a wire rack. Once cooled, use an apple corer to remove a section of sponge from the centre of each cupcake, making sure not to go all the way through, otherwise the filling will dribble out when the case is removed. Pile in a teaspoon or two of the peach/schnapps mixture.

Champagne buttercream:
1. Beat the butter with an electric whisk until light and fluffy. Sieve the icing sugar into the butter, and fold together using a flat knife.
2. Once most of the icing sugar has been incorporated, finish beating with the whisk to combine fully.
3. Add the champagne a tablespoon at a time, beating well between each addition to avoid curdling. Fold in a touch of peach food colouring if required, to give a lovely peachy shade to the buttercream.

BELLINI

1 SIMPLY CHAMPAGNE

Popping candy

The popping candy fizzing on your tongue is almost as good as the real thing. Using a large star nozzle, pipe a swirl of champagne buttercream onto each cupcake and sprinkle with popping candy – simple, but very effective!

BELLINI

2 CARAMELISED PEACHES

Fresh peach slices
Icing sugar to dredge
Tiny white sugar balls (non-pareils)

To caramelise a peach slice, cut one or two peaches in half, and then into slices approx 1 cm thick, dredge with icing sugar and sauté in a hot frying pan until browned. Remove from pan, place on greaseproof paper and allow to cool completely.

Pipe a swirl of champagne buttercream onto each cupcake, then roll the edge of the cupcake in a flat dish of small white sprinkles to create a sugared rim. Top with a beautifully soft caramelised peach slice for extra flavour.

BELLINI

3 DESSERT A DEUX

Popping candy
Champagne flutes

This one's perfect for sharing – and very simple to make. Instead of filling the centres with the peach mix, cut two cupcakes in half horizontally, then cut a circle the same diameter as your glass from the centre of each slice. Drop the first round of cake into the bottom of a glass, add 1-2 teaspoons of the boozy peach filling and top with a swirl of champagne buttercream. Repeat for the remaining rounds, finishing with a peaked swirl of buttercream and a scattering of popping candy. Serve with a long handled spoon – the perfect end to a romantic dinner for two.

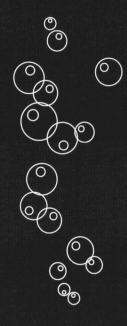

BETWEEN THE SHEETS

THESE DELICIOUS BRANDY AND ORANGE FLAVOURED CUPCAKES ARE AN EXCELLENT SOURCE OF ENERGY FOR ANY ACTIVITY. THEY'LL GO DOWN A STORM AT HEN AND STAG PARTIES – OR ANY ADULT ONLY EVENTS.

preparation time:
25 minutes

cooking time:
24 minutes

Makes 12 cupcakes

i

Cupcakes:
115g unsalted butter (softened)
270g caster sugar
3 medium eggs
225g self raising flour (sifted)
100ml Triple Sec
75g orange curd } mixed

Brandy crunch buttercream:
250g unsalted butter (softened)
275g icing sugar
150g golden caster sugar
120ml brandy
Piping bag with large round or
    star nozzle

m

1. Preheat the oven to 180ºC (160ºC fan).
2. Cream the butter and sugar until light and fluffy.
3. Add the eggs one at a time, beating well
   in-between each egg to avoid curdling.
   Beat in one third of the flour, followed by half
   the orange curd/alcohol mix, and beat until
   fully incorporated. Repeat, then finish with the
   remaining flour.
4. Fill the cupcake cases two thirds full and bake in
   the centre of the oven for 24 minutes, or until a
   skewer inserted in the middle of a cupcake comes
   out clean.
5. Once cooked, allow the cakes to cool in the tin for
   5 minutes, then remove and continue to cool on a
   wire rack.

Brandy crunch buttercream:

1. Beat the butter and caster sugar with an electric
   whisk until light and fluffy. Sieve the icing sugar
   into the butter, add the brandy and fold together
   using a flat knife.
2. Once most of the icing sugar has been
   incorporated, finish beating with the whisk to
   combine fully.

BETWEEN THE SHEETS

1 DO NOT DISTURB!

1 quantity vanilla cookie
  dough (see p154)
Rectangular cookie cutter
  (or easily cut by hand)
White sugarpaste
  (approx 100g)

Small paintbrush
Red edible pen or 2 tbsp red
  royal icing in a piping bag
  fitted with a No. 1 nozzle
  (see p156)

Make the cookie signs using the recipe on p154 and the
rectangular cutter. Bake for approximately 6-8 minutes
until golden.

Once cool, roll out the sugarpaste and cut 12 rectangles the
same size as the cookies. Moisten the cookies with a barely
damp paintbrush and lay the sugarpaste rectangles on top.
Write "Do Not Disturb" (or whatever cheeky message you
fancy) onto each cookie using the edible pen or pipe using the
royal icing. Pipe a swirl of brandy crunch buttercream on each
cupcake using a large star nozzle, and top with a cookie.

IT'S YOUR LUCKY NIGHT

OPEN TO OFFERS!

T B!

BETWEEN THE SHEETS

2 UNBRIDLED PASSION

Pink sugarpaste (approx 100g)
Grey sugarpaste (approx 40g)
Silver edible paint or silver edible dust mixed with a little water
Edible glue

For each pair of handcuffs, roll two thin sausages from the pink sugarpaste, each approximately 7cm long and form into horseshoe shapes. Snip all over with a small sharp pair of scissors to make them look fluffy. From the grey sugarpaste, roll a thin sausage approximately 3cm long and snip to resemble a chain. Also, make two tiny cubes for the locks. Paint these with the silver edible paint or edible dust. Attach the handcuffs to the locks and chain using edible glue and leave to dry for a few minutes.

Pipe a swirl of brandy crunch buttercream on each cupcake using a large star nozzle, and top with a pair of handcuffs. Kinky!

CAKETAILS

BETWEEN THE SHEETS

3 LOVE IN THE AFTERNOON

White sugarpaste (approx 250g)
Black sugarpaste (approx 20g)   } or whatever
Yellow sugarpaste (approx 20g) } colours you prefer
Mini bikini mould (see stockists p157)
icing sugar to dredge

Dredge your work surface liberally with icing sugar, roll out the white sugarpaste as thinly as possible without tearing and cut 12 rectangles roughly the same size as your cupcakes. Bunch up slightly to resemble a rumpled sheet and allow to dry for an hour or so if possible. Make the bras and knickers using tiny amounts of black sugarpaste in the bikini mould. Roll out the yellow sugarpaste and cut 12 pairs of boxer shorts with a sharp knife. This is easily done by cutting small rectangles and removing a wedge out of one of the longer sides.

Pipe a swirl of brandy crunch buttercream on each cupcake, and top with a sheet. Toss the underwear seductively on top of the sheet (and fix with a dab of water).

39

BLUSHING GEISHA

THE DELICATE ROSE FLAVOUR OF THIS CUPCAKE REFLECTS THE UNIQUE FEMININITY OF THE GEISHA. AND JUST LIKE THE GEISHA, IT HAS HIDDEN FIRE INSIDE.

preparation time:
25 minutes

cooking time:
24 minutes

Makes 12 cupcakes

i

Cupcakes:
165g unsalted butter (softened)
180g caster sugar
3 medium eggs
175g self raising flour (sifted)
40ml sake
40ml pomegranate molasses
Pink paste food colouring
Dried crystallised rose petals
(approx 10g) for sprinkling
3-4 tbsp sake for drizzling

Rose buttercream:
250g unsalted butter (softened)
500g icing sugar
¾ tsp rose essence
Touch of pink paste
   food colouring
Piping bag with large round or
   star nozzle

m

1. Preheat the oven to 180°C (160°C fan).
2. Mix together the sake, pomegranate molasses and pink food colouring and set aside
3. Cream the butter and sugar until light and fluffy
4. Add the eggs one at a time, beating well in-between each egg to avoid curdling. Beat in half the flour, followed by the sake mixture, and beat until fully incorporated. Finish with the remaining flour.
5. Fill the cupcake cases half full, scatter a few crystallised rose petals on top of each cupcake and bake in the centre of the oven for 24 minutes, or until a skewer inserted in the middle of a cupcake comes out clean.
6. Once cooked, allow the cakes to cool in the tin for 5 minutes, then remove and continue to cool on a wire rack.
7. Once cool, make holes in the top of each cupcake using a skewer, and drizzle generously with sake.

Rose buttercream:

1. Beat the butter with an electric whisk until light and fluffy. Sieve the icing sugar into the butter, add the rose essence and a touch of pink paste food colouring and fold together using a flat knife.
2. Once most of the icing sugar has been incorporated, finish beating with the whisk to combine fully.

BLUSHING GEISHA

1 JEWELLED DELIGHT

Pomegranate seeds

Pipe a swirl of rose buttercream on each cupcake using a star nozzle, and liberally scatter with pomegranate seeds.

BLUSHING GEISHA

2 GEISHA GIRL

Black and white sugarpaste (approx 180g of each)
Red sugarpaste (approx 10g)
Tiny blossom cutter
Tiny heart cutter or heart shaped sprinkles

Small circle cutter (approx 2cm diameter)
Larger circle cutter (the same diameter as your cupcakes)
Small paintbrush

Dredge your work surface liberally with icing sugar, roll out the white sugarpaste and cut 12 large circles, then repeat with the black sugarpaste. Use the template on page 165 to cut a shape for the hair from each black circle. Use some of the remaining black paste to cut 12 smaller black circles. Use a dab of water to fix these to the top of each white circle to make the bun. Next, dampen the top half and sides of the white circles, and place the black hair shapes on top.

From the remaining black sugarpaste, cut 24 thin crescents using the small circle cutter. Position these on the white face for downcast eyes, securing with the tiniest dab of water. Cut 12 tiny hearts from the red sugarpaste, and use for the lips (or heart shaped sprinkles will do the job just as well). Also cut 12 tiny red blossoms, and position one on each bun. Finally, spread a layer of rose buttercream onto each cupcake up to the level of the case, and gently lay the geisha face on top.

BLUSHING GEISHA

3 CHERRY BLOSSOM

Brown sugarpaste (approx 120g)
White sugarpaste (approx 50g)
Blossom cutters (assorted sizes)
Small paintbrush
Pink edible dust
2 tbsp dark pink royal icing in a piping bag with No.2 nozzle (see p156)
Large piping bag with large round nozzle

Use the brown sugarpaste to make 12 forked branches. Roll out the white sugarpaste, and cut a variety of different sized blossoms (approx 10-12 per branch). Use the paintbrush to dust the inside of each blossom with pink dust, and then pipe small dots of pink royal icing inside each blossom for the centres. Use the remaining pink royal icing to secure each blossom to its branch in a random pattern. Pipe a swirl of rose buttercream on each cupcake, then decorate with a branch of cherry blossom.

SEX ON THE BEACH

THESE FRUITY LITTLE CUPCAKES ARE ONLY A LITTLE BIT NAUGHTY, BUT DEFINITELY VERY NICE!

preparation time:
25 minutes excluding soaking time

cooking time:
24 minutes

Makes 12 cupcakes

i

Cupcakes:
115g unsalted butter (softened)
270g caster sugar
3 medium eggs
225g self raising flour (sifted)
75g dried cranberries
75ml vodka
75ml peach schnapps

Cassis buttercream:
250g unsalted butter (softened)
500g icing sugar
125ml crème de cassis liqueur
Grated zest of 2 oranges
Large piping bag with large
    round or star nozzle

1. Soak the cranberries in the vodka and peach schnapps for a couple of hours or overnight to soften and swell.
2. Preheat the oven to 180ºC (160ºC fan).
3. Cream the butter and sugar until light and fluffy.
4. Add the eggs one at a time, beating well in-between each egg to avoid curdling. Beat in one third of the flour, followed by half the cranberry/alcohol mix, and beat until fully incorporated. Repeat, then finish with the remaining flour.
5. Fill the cupcake cases two thirds full and bake in the centre of the oven for 24 minutes, or until a skewer inserted in the middle of a cupcake comes out clean.
6. Once cooked, allow the cakes to cool in the tin for 5 minutes, then remove and continue to cool on a wire rack.

Cassis buttercream:
1. Beat the butter with an electric whisk until light and fluffy. Sieve the icing sugar into the butter, add the cassis and fold together using a flat knife.
2. Once most of the icing sugar has been incorporated, finish beating with the whisk to combine fully, then gently fold in the orange zest.

SEX ON THE BEACH

1 HELLO CHEEKY

Silicone bum mould
  (see stockists p157)
Light brown sugarpaste
  (approx 100g)
2 tbsp blue royal icing
  in a bag with a
  No. 2 nozzle (see p156)

Golden caster sugar for
  sprinkling
Icing sugar to dust
Pink & orange paste food
  colouring

To make the bums, first dust the mould with icing sugar
to prevent the sugarpaste from sticking, then firmly press
sugarpaste into the mould. Remove any excess using a sharp
knife. Remove the bum by gently twisting the mould. Pipe
a thong with the royal icing, following the lines impressed
by the mould. Immediately sprinkle caster sugar onto bum
cheeks and upper thigh to resemble sand.

Add pink and orange food colouring to the buttercream and
partly mix to give ribbons of colour. Pipe a swirl of cassis
buttercream on each cupcake using a large star nozzle and
place bum cheekily on top!

SEX ON THE BEACH

2 GINGERBREAD LOVERS

1 quantity Guinness gingerbread cookie dough (see p155)
Small gingerbread man cutter or template on p165
Edible pens (red and black)
1 tbsp each of pink and orange royal icing in piping bags
    fitted with No.2 nozzles (or any colour of your choice)
    (see p156)
Pink edible glitter
Blue food colouring
Digestive biscuits – crushed (approx 2-3)

Make 24 gingerbread men cookies using the recipe on
p155. Before baking, use the offcuts to make 24 small
balls, and place two in the appropriate place on 12 of the
gingerbread men to make them into ladies. If you want to
be totally authentic, roll a tiny (or not so tiny!) sausage for
the men, and position accordingly. Bake for approx
5 minutes, until just beginning to brown. Allow to cool
completely before decorating.

Draw faces onto the figures using the edible pens, and
pipe swimwear with the royal icing. Colour the cassis
buttercream blue, then spread generously over each
cupcake. Sprinkle crushed digestive biscuits over half the
icing to make sand, and push both gingerbread people into
the sandy side of the cake.

SEX ON THE BEACH

3 FUN IN THE SUN

Candy beach balls
Cocktail umbrellas
Orange and yellow sugarpaste (approx 50g of each)
Small rectangular cutter

To make the towels, first roll the orange sugarpaste into a long thin tube, and then flatten using a rolling pin, to give a strip approx 5x26cms. Repeat for the yellow sugarpaste, then cut this horizontally into thin strips approximately 5cm long by ½cm wide. Lay the yellow strips perpendicularly across the long orange strip, and roll gently with a rolling pin to fix the yellow into the orange. Cut into 12 towel shapes, approx 2x4cms, using a rectangular cutter or a sharp knife. Finally, use very small scissors or a sharp knife to snip a fringe either end of the towel.

Pipe a swirl of cassis buttercream on each cupcake using a large round nozzle and decorate with a towel, a candy ball and a cocktail umbrella.

BLACK VELVET

THIS IS A REAL MAN'S CAKETAIL — THE RUGGEDNESS OF GUINNESS, COMBINED WITH THE SMOOTHNESS OF CHAMPAGNE. IF ONLY ALL MEN COULD BE LIKE THIS CAKETAIL!

preparation time:
20 minutes

cooking time:
24 minutes

Makes 12 cupcakes

i

Cupcakes:
160ml Guinness
160g unsalted butter
60g cocoa
330g caster sugar
2 medium eggs
65ml sour cream
½ tsp vanilla extract
200g plain flour (sifted)
1½ tsp bicarbonate of soda
  (sifted)

Champagne cream:
800ml double cream
200ml champagne
160g icing sugar
Piping bag with large round
  nozzle

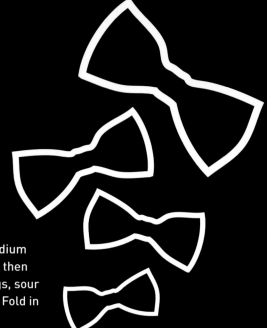
m

1. Preheat the oven to 180°C (160°C fan).
2. Gently heat the Guinness and butter together in a medium saucepan until melted. Whisk in the cocoa and sugar, then allow to cool for a few minutes. Beat together the eggs, sour cream and vanilla and stir into the Guinness mixture. Fold in the flour and bicarbonate of soda until incorporated.
3. Fill the cupcake cases two thirds full and bake in the centre of the oven for 24 minutes, or until a skewer inserted in the middle of a cupcake comes out clean.
4. Once cooked, allow the cakes to cool in the tin for 5 minutes, then remove and continue to cool on a wire rack.

Champagne cream:
Whisk the cream, champagne and icing sugar together until soft peaks form. This is best eaten immediately.

BLACK VELVET

1 BLACK GOLD

Using a large round nozzle, pipe a flat swirl
of champagne cream onto each cupcake –
smooth...rich.... dark; its so like a pint of
Guinness, its uncanny.

CAKETAILS

BLACK VELVET

2 CHOCOLATE TRUFFLES

80ml double cream
40g dark chocolate (min 50%)
40g milk chocolate
Cocoa powder to dredge
Chocolate sprinkles

To make the truffles, break the chocolate into a heatproof bowl. Pour the cream into a small saucepan and bring to the boil. Remove from the heat and pour immediately over the chocolate, stirring continuously until melted and glossy. Place in the fridge to set for 30–45 minutes.

Roll teaspoonfuls of the truffle mixture into balls using the palms of your hands and then roll each ball in cocoa powder. Store in the fridge until needed.

Pipe a swirl of champagne cream onto each cupcake, top with a truffle and scatter sprinkles around the edges.

3 MINE'S A PINT!

1 quantity of Guinness gingerbread cookie dough (see p155)
Pint glass template (see p164)
100g dark chocolate
50g white chocolate

COOKIES

Make the gingerbread cookies using the recipe on p155 and the pint glass template. Bake for approx 6-8 minutes until golden.

Once cool, melt 100g dark chocolate in a small bowl, spoon melted chocolate over most of the cookie, leaving approx 1 cm bare at the top. Do this on a wire rack, so any excess drips through onto a piece of baking parchment.

Once the dark chocolate has set, repeat the process with 50g of white chocolate to give the famous Guinness top. Allow to dry completely.

Pipe a flat swirl of champagne cream onto each cupcake and finish with a Guinness gingerbread cookie – 2 treats for the price of one!

BLACK VELVET

COSMOPOLITAN

CARRIE BRADSHAW'S TWO FAVOURITE THINGS ARE COSMOPOLITANS AND CUPCAKES — WE'RE SURE SHE'D QUEUE ROUND THE BLOCK FOR THIS SOPHISTICATED CAKETAIL, WHICH COMBINES BOTH IN A GLORIOUS MOUTHFUL OF PLEASURE.

preparation time:
20 minutes, excluding soaking time

cooking time:
24 minutes

Makes 12 cupcakes

i

Cupcakes:
115g unsalted butter (softened)
270g caster sugar
3 medium eggs
225g self raising flour (sifted)
75g dried cranberries
75ml vodka
75ml Cointreau
3-4 tbsp Cointreau for drizzling

Cointreau buttercream:
250g unsalted butter (softened)
500g icing sugar
100ml Cointreau
Grated zest of 1 lime
Pink paste food colouring
Piping bag with large round or
    leaf nozzle

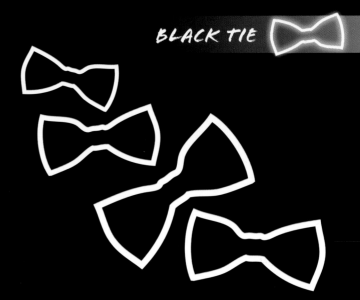
m

1. Soak the cranberries in the vodka and Cointreau for a couple of hours or overnight to soften and swell.
2. Preheat the oven to 180ºC (160ºC fan).
3. Cream the butter and sugar until light and fluffy.
4. Add the eggs one at a time, beating well in-between each egg to avoid curdling. Beat in one third of the flour, followed by half the cranberry/alcohol mix, and beat until fully incorporated. Repeat, then finish with the remaining flour.
5. Fill the cupcake cases two thirds full and bake in the centre of the oven for 24 minutes, or until a skewer inserted in the middle of a cupcake comes out clean.
6. Once cooked, allow the cakes to cool in the tin for 5 minutes, then remove and continue to cool on a wire rack. Make holes in the top of each cupcake using a fork or skewer and drizzle generously with Cointreau.

Cointreau buttercream:

1. Beat the butter with an electric whisk until light and fluffy. Sieve the icing sugar into the butter, add the Cointreau and fold together using a flat knife.
2. Once most of the icing sugar has been incorporated, finish beating with the whisk to combine fully.
3. Add a touch of pink food colouring and the lime zest and fold in gently with a spatula to give a marbled effect.

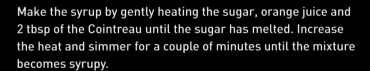

1 ORANGE DRIZZLE

50g caster sugar
2 tbsp orange juice
3 tbsp Cointreau
Gold sugar balls

Make the syrup by gently heating the sugar, orange juice and
2 tbsp of the Cointreau until the sugar has melted. Increase
the heat and simmer for a couple of minutes until the mixture
becomes syrupy.

Remove from the heat and add the remaining Cointreau
(don't worry of it appears thin at this stage – it will continue to
thicken as it cools).

Pipe a swirl of Cointreau buttercream onto each cupcake using a
large round nozzle then drizzle syrup liberally over the cupcakes,
allowing it to run down the sides for added decadence. If the syrup
becomes too thick, add a little more Cointreau or orange juice
to loosen.

COSMOPOLITAN

2 *PURE DECADENCE*

Edible gold leaf

Pipe a swirl of Cointreau buttercream
onto each cupcake, and decorate
with small pieces of gold leaf – fiddly,
but worth the effort (tweezers and a
cocktail stick are good for this.)

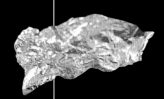

COSMOPOLITAN

3 HEART TO HEART

Pink and orange sugarpaste
  (approx 50g of each)
Heart cutters (small & medium)
Edible glue
Pink and orange edible glitter

Cut an assortment of hearts from
the pink and orange sugarpastes,
sprinkle both with glitter (see p6.) Glue
together using a dab of buttercream or
edible glue. Pipe a swirl of Cointreau
buttercream onto each cupcake and
decorate with glittered hearts.

MARTINI

ELEGANT AND UNDERSTATED – THIS CAKETAIL IS THE EPITOME OF SUAVE AND SOPHISTICATION. JAMES BOND – EAT YOUR HEART OUT!

preparation time:
30 minutes

cooking time:
22-24 minutes

Makes 12 cupcakes

i

Cupcakes:
165g unsalted butter (softened)
165g caster sugar
3 medium eggs
165g self raising flour (sifted)
45ml vodka
3-4 tbsp vodka for drizzling

To fill:
50g lemon curd
10ml vodka } mixed
Apple corer

Vermouth glace icing:
500g icing sugar (sieved)
85-90ml vermouth

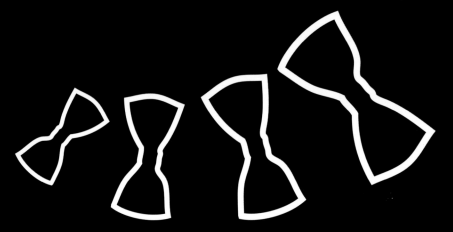

m

1. Preheat the oven to 180°C (160°C fan).
2. Cream the butter and sugar until light and fluffy.
3. Add the eggs one at a time, beating well in-between each egg to avoid curdling. Beat in one third of the flour, followed by half the vodka, and beat until fully incorporated. Repeat , finishing with the remaining flour.
4. Fill the cupcake cases half full and bake in the centre of the oven for 22-24 minutes, or until a skewer inserted in the middle of a cupcake comes out clean. Don't overfill the cupcake cases, as you'll need to leave some space at the top to hold the glace icing.
5. Once cooked, allow the cakes to cool in the tin for 5 minutes, then remove and continue to cool on a wire rack. Once cooled, trim off the centre of the cupcakes if they've peaked, and make holes in the top using a skewer. Drizzle generously with vodka.
6. Use an apple corer to remove a section of sponge from the centre of each cupcake, making sure not to go right through to the bottom, otherwise your filling will spill out as soon as the wrapper is taken off. Fill the cavity with a teaspoon or two of the vodka/lemon curd mix, then use a thin slice of the removed core to seal the filling in (otherwise the lemon curd may discolour the white glace icing.)

Vermouth glace icing:
Mix the icing sugar with the vermouth until it is the consistency of thick double cream. Add more vermouth or icing sugar as necessary. If not using immediately, cover the icing tightly with cling film to prevent crusting.

MARTINI

1 LEMON TWISTS

Lemon peel cut into long thin strips,
lightly brushed with water and
sprinkled with caster sugar

Spoon vermouth glace icing over the
cupcake, up to the level of the rim of
the case. Allow to set, then add a twist
of sugared lemon peel. Not shaken or
stirred, but very, very classy!

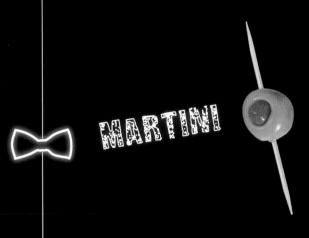

MARTINI

2 SWEET OLIVES

Green sugarpaste (approx 100g)
6 red jellybeans
Cocktail sticks

Spoon vermouth glace icing over the
cupcakes up to the level of the rims of the
cases, and allow to set. Roll small oval
shapes from the green sugarpaste to make
the olives. Cut red jelly beans in half, and
push gently – cut sides inwards – into one
end of each olive. Insert cocktail sticks
through the middle of the olives, and place
across the top of each cupcake – looks just
like the real thing.

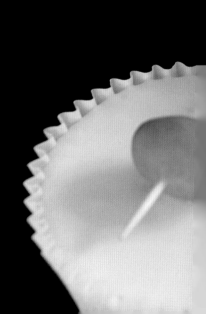

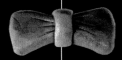

MARTINI

3 ALL DRESSED UP

Black sugarpaste (approx 100g)
White sugar balls

Spoon vermouth glace icing over the cupcake,
up to the level of the rim of the case and allow
to set. Make the bow tie by moulding a small
piece of black sugarpaste into two triangles,
adding a strip around the centre to finish. Place
at the top of each cupcake, and add 3 white sugar
balls underneath as buttons – the height of
sophistication and glamour.

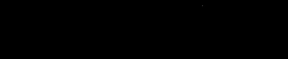

BLUE LAGOON

THE BRIGHT BLUE OF THIS CUPCAKE BELIES ITS TANGY ORANGE FLAVOUR- AND THE VODKA SOAKED PINEAPPLE INSIDE IS THE PERFECT SURPRISE.

preparation time:
25 minutes excluding soaking time

cooking time:
22-24 minutes

Makes 12 cupcakes

Cupcakes:
165g unsalted butter (softened)
165g caster sugar
3 medium eggs
220g self raising flour (sifted)
150ml vodka
200g finely chopped dried pineapple
50ml Blue Curaçao
3-4 tbsp Blue Curaçao for drizzling
Blue food colouring (optional)

] buttercream:
250g unsalted butter (softened)
500g icing sugar
120ml Blue Curaçao
Grated rind of 1 large orange
Blue food colouring
Large piping bag fitted with large round or star nozzle

m

1. Place the chopped dried pineapple into a small bowl with the vodka and set aside to soak for an hour or two, until most of the vodka has been absorbed.
2. Preheat the oven to 180°C (160°C fan).
3. Cream the butter and sugar until light and fluffy.
4. Add the eggs one at a time, beating well in-between each egg to avoid curdling. Beat in one third of the flour, followed by 25ml Blue Curaçao (and blue food colouring if desired), and beat until fully incorporated. Repeat, finishing with the remaining flour. Fold in the soaked pineapple, and any remaining vodka.
5. Fill the cupcake cases two thirds full and bake in the centre of the oven for 24 minutes, or until a skewer inserted in the middle of a cupcake comes out clean.
6. Once cooked, allow the cakes to cool in the tin for 5 minutes, then remove and continue to cool on a wire rack. Once cooled, make holes in the top of each cupcake using a fork or skewer, and drizzle with the remaining Blue Curaçao.

Curaçao buttercream:

1. Beat the butter with an electric whisk until light and fluffy. Sieve the icing sugar into the butter, add the Curaçao and fold together using a flat knife.
2. Once most of the icing sugar has been incorporated, finish beating with the whisk to combine fully.
3. Add blue food colouring and the orange zest and mix briefly with a spatula to give a marbled effect.

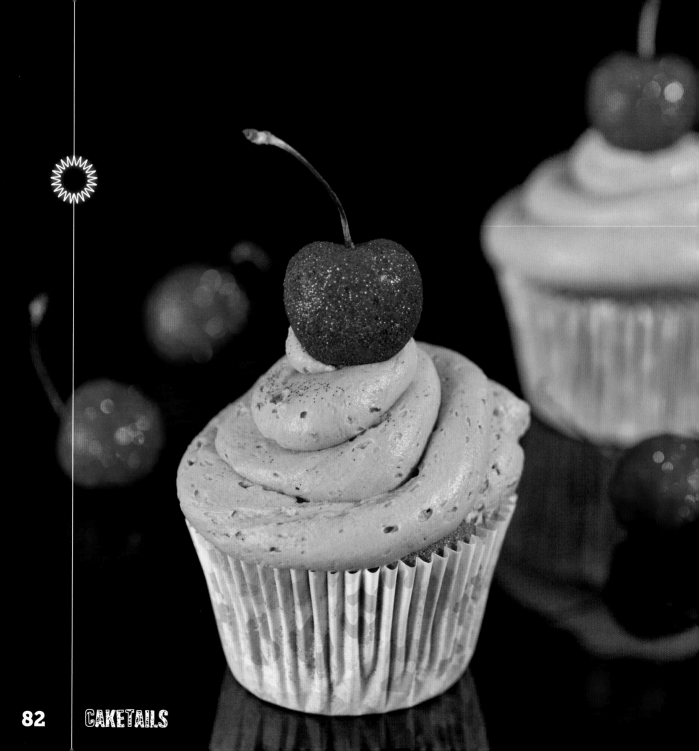

BLUE LAGOON

1 GLITZY CHERRIES

Fresh cherries
edible glue
Red edible glitter
Paintbrush

To glitter the cherries, paint a fresh
cherry with edible glue and sprinkle
liberally with edible glitter (see p6).

Pipe a swirl of Curaçao buttercream onto
each cupcake using a large round nozzle
and top with a stunning glittered cherry.

BLUE LAGOON

2 VODKA JELLIES

Citrus segment mould (see stockists p157)
35g orange flavoured jelly cubes
25ml boiling water
100ml vodka
Vegetable oil to grease

These boozy vodka jelly segments are a really fun decoration – but make sure you put them on at the last minute, as they have a tendency to wobble off!

Make the vodka jelly at least 4 hours before you want to decorate your cupcakes, and preferably the night before, as it will need time to set fully.

To make, break up the cubes of jelly in a jug and pour in the boiling water. Stir until dissolved, then add the vodka and stir. Grease the moulds with a tiny amount of vegetable oil, then pour the jelly into the moulds. Refrigerate until completely set. Don't try to freeze these for a speedier set – all the vodka evaporates!

Pipe a swirl of Curaçao buttercream onto each cupcake and top with a jelly.

3 MARINE LIFE

1 quantity vanilla cookie dough (see p154)
Dolphin cookie cutter (or use template on p164)
2 quantities royal icing (see p156)
3 small piping bags fitted with No. 2 nozzles
Black food colouring

COOKIES

Make the dolphin cookies using the recipe on p154 and the dolphin
cutter or template. Bake for 6-8 minutes until golden.

Whilst these are cooling, colour 460g of royal icing pale grey and
60g black, leaving 60g white. Spoon 60g of the pale grey icing into a
piping bag fitted with a No.2 nozzle and pipe an outline around each
dolphin cookie. Allow to dry for 10-15 minutes.

Place the remaining grey icing into a small bowl, and loosen with
drops of water until it reaches the consistency of thick double
cream. Spoon this into a new piping bag without a nozzle, snip off
the very tip and flood the cookies until each dolphin is completely
grey. Once dry, pipe a smile on each dolphin using the white royal
icing, and an eye using the black royal icing – both in piping bags
with No. 2 nozzles.

Pipe waves of Curaçao buttercream on each cupcake using a star
nozzle, and top with a dolphin cookie.

For a fun finish, garnish with fish cut from orange peel.

MOJITO

TO US, MINT ALWAYS CONJURES UP THE SMELL OF SUMMER – AND COMBINED WITH RUM AND LIME, A MOJITO IS ONE OF OUR FAVOURITE SUMMER COCKTAILS – AND NOW, ONE OF OUR FAVOURITE CAKETAILS TOO!

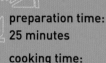

preparation time:
25 minutes

cooking time:
24 minutes

Makes 12 cupcakes

i

Cupcakes:
165g unsalted butter (softened)
165g caster sugar
3 medium eggs
165g self raising flour (sifted)
50ml white rum
Zest of 1 lime
Finely chopped mint (about
   15 leaves)
3-4 tbsp crème de menthe
   for drizzling

Rum buttercream:
250g unsalted butter (softened)
500g icing sugar
85ml white rum
30ml crème de menthe
Piping bag with large round or
   star nozzle

m

1. Preheat the oven to 180ºC (160ºC fan).
2. Cream the butter and sugar until light and fluffy.
3. Add the eggs one at a time, beating well in-between each egg to avoid curdling. Beat in one third of the flour, followed by half the rum, and beat until fully incorporated. Repeat, finishing with the remaining flour. Fold in the lime zest and chopped mint.
4. Fill the cupcake cases two thirds full and bake in the centre of the oven for 24 minutes, or until a skewer inserted in the middle of a cupcake comes out clean.
5. Once cooked, allow the cakes to cool in the tin for 5 minutes, then remove and continue to cool on a wire rack. Make holes in the top of each cupcake using a skewer, and drizzle with crème de menthe.

Rum buttercream:
1. Beat the butter with an electric whisk until light and fluffy. Sieve the icing sugar into the butter, add the rum and crème de menthe and fold together using a flat knife.
2. Once most of the icing sugar has been incorporated, finish beating with the whisk to combine fully.

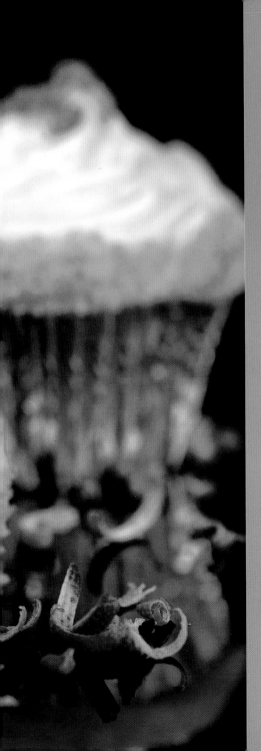

MOJITO

1 PURE & SIMPLE

Green sanding sugar
Lime zest

Use a large star nozzle to pipe a swirl of rum buttercream onto each cupcake, roll the edges in sanding sugar and finish with a sprinkling of julienned lime zest. These cupcakes look very stylish presented in silver cupcake cases, with wedges of juicy lime to garnish.

MOJITO

2 CLEARLY MINTY

12 Clear mint sweets
12 small perfect mint leaves

Preheat the oven to 140°C (120°C fan), then evenly space the mint leaves on a large baking tray lined with reusable baking parchment.

Place a clear mint sweet directly on top of each leaf and pop in the oven for 5 minutes or so, until each sweet has melted, encasing each mint leaf in its own tiny clear disc. Do make sure there is enough space between the sweets before baking, as they spread quite a lot once melted, and keep a close eye on them, as its very easy for the mint leaves to burn.

Remove from the oven and allow to cool and harden completely before removing from the baking parchment. Also, try not to touch the sweets except on the edges, as they do pick up fingermarks very easily.

Pipe a swirl of rum buttercream on each cupcake and top with the mint disc.

MOJITO

3 CHOCOLATE MINT LEAVES

White, milk or dark chocolate (approx 100g)
zest of 1 lime
Small leaf cutter

Melt the chocolate using a microwave or bain marie, then pour directly onto a baking tray lined with non-stick baking parchment.

Tip the tray to spread the chocolate evenly and thinly. Refrigerate for 5-10 minutes or until firm to the touch then remove and cut leaf shapes into the chocolate using the cutter.

Do not try to remove them at this point. Return to the fridge for a further 30 minutes or so until hardened completely, then carefully snap around the leaves to remove them, and store in the fridge until needed.

Pipe a swirl of rum buttercream on each cupcake, and top with a chocolate leaf and some grated lime zest.

PINA COLADA

THIS IS THE ULTIMATE SUMMER COCKTAIL – CONJURING UP BEACHES AND PALM TREES AND GLORIOUS SUNSHINE. THE FLAVOURS OF A PINA COLADA – COCONUT, RUM AND PINEAPPLE – TAKE US RIGHT BACK TO CARIBBEAN HOLIDAYS AND LAZY SUMMER DAYS – FANCY BEING ABLE TO RECREATE THAT FEELING IN YOUR BACK GARDEN WITH A DOZEN CAKETAILS!

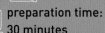

preparation time:
30 minutes

cooking time:
24 minutes

Makes 12 cupcakes

i

Caketails:
75g unsalted butter (softened)
180g caster sugar
2 medium eggs
150g self raising flour (sifted)
50ml Malibu
100ml coconut milk ⎫ mixed
40ml pineapple juice ⎭
100g chopped tinned pineapple
  (drained)
60g desiccated coconut

Coconut rum buttercream:
250g unsalted butter (softened)
500g icing sugar
60ml white rum
60g toasted coconut
Large piping bags with large
  round or star nozzles

1. Preheat the oven to 180ºC (160ºC fan).
2. Toast the coconut in a dry frying pan over a gentle heat for a few minutes, stirring constantly to avoid burning. Set aside to cool.
3. Cream the butter and sugar until light and fluffy.
4. Add the eggs one at a time, beating well in-between each egg to avoid curdling. Toss the pineapple in a small amount of the flour to prevent it sinking to the bottom of the cupcakes during cooking. Beat in one third of the remaining flour, followed by half the Malibu mixture, and beat until fully incorporated. Repeat, finishing with the rest of the flour. Fold in the toasted coconut and chopped pineapple.

5. Fill the cupcake cases two thirds full and bake in the centre of the oven for 24 minutes, or until a skewer inserted in the middle of a cupcake comes out clean.
6. Once cooked, allow the cakes to cool in the tin for 5 minutes, then remove and continue to cool on a wire rack.

Coconut rum buttercream:

1. Beat the butter with an electric whisk until light and fluffy. Sieve the icing sugar into the butter, add the rum and and fold using a flat knife.
2. Once most of the icing sugar has been incorporated, finish beating with the whisk to combine fully.
3. Finally, gently fold in the toasted coconut.

PINA COLADA

1 FRESH & FRUITY

Fresh pineapple
Maraschino cherries

Pipe a swirl of buttercream onto each cupcake using a large star nozzle, then chop up some fresh pineapple and pile a little golden cluster on top of each swirl, topping with a maraschino cherry. These look mouthwatering displayed on piles of fragrant coconut – perfect for a summer party.

PINA COLADA

2 PERFECT PINEAPPLES

Milk chocolate (approx 100g)
Small pineapple cutter
Edible glitter (orange and green)

To make the pineapples:
1. Melt the chocolate using a microwave or bain marie. Using a flat knife, spread a couple of rectangles approx 7.5cm wide and 25.5cm long onto a baking sheet lined with non-stick baking parchment.
2. Pop in the fridge for 5 minutes to half set, then sprinkle green glitter in a strip along the top long edge of the chocolate (approx 2.5cm deep), and then a strip of orange glitter beneath (approx 5cm deep). Impress diagonal lines into the orange strip using a knife to make a diamond pattern.
3. Place back in the fridge for a further 10–15 minutes, then remove, and cut pineapple shapes using a small cookie cutter into the chocolate, lining up the leaves with the green glitter, and the pineapple with the orange glitter.
4. Replace in the fridge to harden completely (around half an hour or so), then gently ease the pineapples off the parchment and set aside. If the chocolate's set really well, you can 'snap' the shapes out if you go round carefully.

Pipe a swirl of coconut rum buttercream on each cupcake and decorate with a chocolate pineapple.

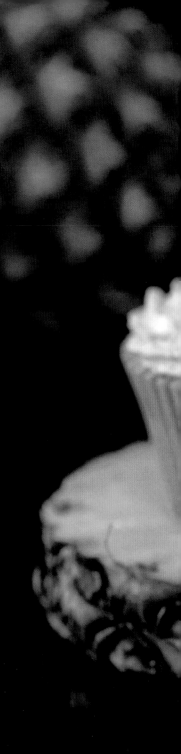

PINA COLADA

3 BEACH PARTY

TO MAKE A REAL IMPRESSION, GO ALL OUT TO RECREATE A CARIBBEAN BEACH — COMPLETE WITH PALM TREES AND COCONUTS (BOTH THE REAL AND CHOCOLATE VARIETY!)

PINA COLADA

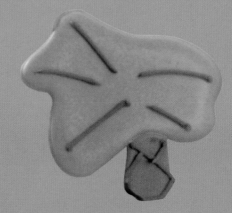

3 BEACH PARTY

Palm tree cookies:

1 quantity vanilla cookie dough (see p 154)
Palm tree cookie cutter or template (see p164)
2 quantities royal icing (see p156)

Coconut truffles:

160ml double cream
80g dark chocolate (min 50%),

80g milk chocolate
60g toasted coconut

PALM TREE COOKIES

1. Make the palm tree cookies using the recipe on p154 and a palm tree cookie cutter or template. Bake for 6-8 minutes until golden.
2. While the cookies are cooling, colour 250g royal icing light green, 250g light brown, 30g dark green and 30g dark brown.
3. Using piping bags with No.2 nozzles, pipe the outline of the foliage of each tree in light green royal icing, and the outline of each trunk in light brown and set aside to dry.
4. While these are drying, cut the nozzles off the light green and light brown piping bags you've just used, and squeeze the remaining icing into two small bowls. Add drops of water to each and stir to thin down the icing to the consistency of thick double cream.
5. Refill two new piping bags (no nozzles this time), snip off the very end of each tip and use these to flood the centres of each tree (the foliage with light green and the trunk with light brown). Flood all the trunks first and after 15 minutes or so, flood the foliage – if you do them too soon, the icing will run at the edges.
6. Once both sections are fully dry, use new bags and clean nozzles to pipe branch lines in dark green on the foliage and criss cross lines in dark brown on the trunk. These cookies can be made a day or two in advance and stored in an airtight tin.

COCONUT TRUFFLES

1. Toast the coconut in a dry frying pan over a gentle heat for a few minutes, stirring constantly to avoid burning. Set aside to cool completely.
2. Meanwhile, break the chocolate into a heatproof bowl. Pour the cream into a small saucepan and bring to the boil. Remove from the heat and pour immediately over the chocolate, stirring continuously until melted and glossy. Place in the fridet for 30–45 minutes.
3. Roll half-teaspoonfuls of the truffle mixture into balls using the palms of your hands and then toss each ball in the toasted coconut. Store in the fridge until needed.

Pipe a deep swirl of coconut rum buttercream onto each cupcake and decorate with a palm tree cookie and 2 or 3 truffles.

ZOMBIE

THIS DARKLY NAMED CUPCAKE TASTES SURPRISINGLY FRESH AND FRUITY. HAVE FUN WITH THE DECORATING — THE MORE GHOULISH AND GRUESOME THE BETTER!

preparation time:
25 minutes excluding soaking time

cooking time:
25 minutes

Makes 12 cupcakes

Cupcakes:
115g unsalted butter (softened)
270g caster sugar
3 medium eggs
225g self raising flour (sifted)
75g chopped dried pineapple
75ml dark rum
75ml apricot brandy

Lime rum buttercream:
250g unsalted butter (softened)
500g icing sugar
120ml dark rum
½ tsp lime juice
Grated zest of 2 limes
Piping bag with large round or
    star nozzle

m

1. Soak the chopped pineapple in the rum and apricot brandy for a couple of hours or overnight to soften and swell.
2. Preheat the oven to 180ºC (160ºC fan).
3. Cream the butter and sugar until light and fluffy.
4. Add the eggs one at a time, beating well in-between each egg to avoid curdling. Beat in one third of the flour, followed by half the pineapple/alcohol mix, and beat until fully incorporated. Repeat , then finish with the remaining flour.
5. Fill the cupcake cases two thirds full and bake in the centre of the oven for 25 minutes, or until a skewer inserted in the middle of a cupcake comes out clean.
6. Once cooked, allow the cakes to cool in the tin for 5 minutes, then remove and continue to cool on a wire rack.

Lime rum buttercream:
1. Beat the butter with an electric whisk until light and fluffy. Sieve the icing sugar into the butter, add the rum and lime juice and fold together using a flat knife.
2. Once most of the icing sugar has been incorporated, finish beating with the whisk to combine fully, then gently fold in the lime zest.

1 BLOODBATH

Glace cherries
Grenadine or strawberry syrup

Pipe a swirl of lime rum buttercream onto each cupcake and top with a glace cherry. Drizzle liberally with grenadine or strawberry syrup.

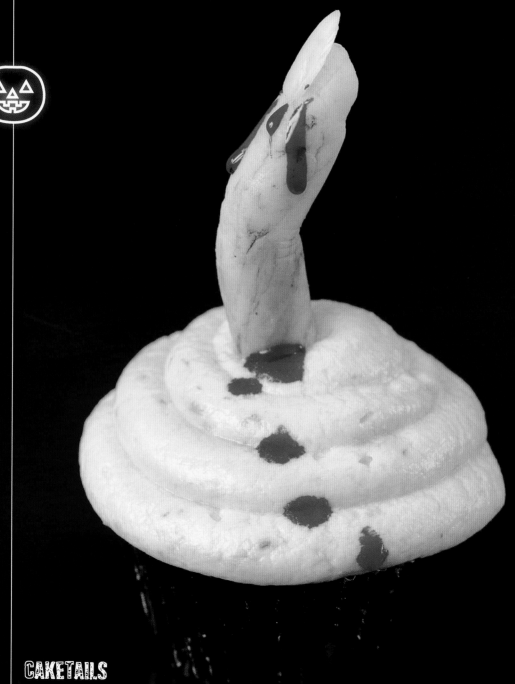

ZOMBIE

2 THE ZOMBIES ARE COMING...

Marzipan (approx 240g)
Flaked almonds
Brown paste food colouring
Edible glue
Cocktail sticks
Strawberry syrup or jam

To make the fingers, add a tiny amount of brown food colouring to the marzipan and knead briefly, leaving streaks of the colour unmixed, for effect. For each cupcake, mould approximately 20g of marzipan into a finger shape. Bend each finger slightly and mark knuckles with a knife then set aside for 20 minutes or so to harden slightly. Stick an almond flake onto the end of each finger with a dab of edible glue for the fingernails, then push a cocktail stick halfway into the bottom of each finger to help secure them to the cake. Drizzle strawberry syrup or jam on the finger to resemble blood.

Pipe a swirl of lime rum buttercream onto each cupcake using a large round nozzle and position the fingers appropriately.

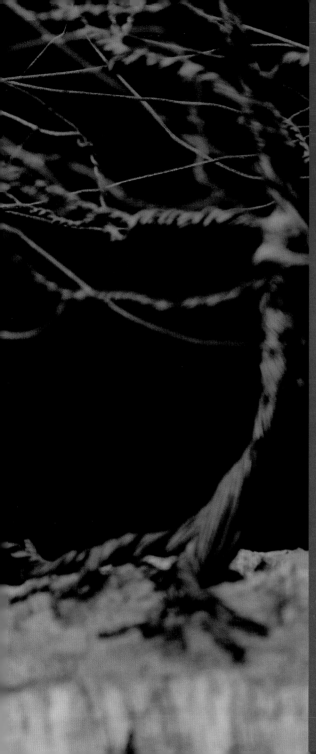

ZOMBIE

3 DEAD EASY

Oreo cookies
Chocolate sticks

Pipe a swirl of lime rum buttercream onto each cupcake using a large round nozzle and make an indentation for the grave in the centre of each with a flat knife. Crumble up the Oreo cookies and use to fill the grave.

Use the chocolate sticks to make crosses, sticking the pieces together with tiny dabs of melted chocolate (melt an extra stick for this). Push the crosses into the cupcakes above the graves and scatter some more cookie crumbs around the holes for disturbed dirt.

RUSTY NAIL

HANDY TO HAVE IN CASE THERE ARE A FEW VAMPIRES ABOUT ON HALLOWEEN. NOT QUITE A STAKE THROUGH THE HEART, BUT SURELY A RUSTY NAIL WOULD DO THE TRICK...?

preparation time:
25 minutes

cooking time:
24 minutes

Makes 12 cupcakes

i

Cupcakes:
115g unsalted butter (softened)
270g caster sugar
3 medium eggs
225g self raising flour (sifted)
125ml Drambuie

Whiskey buttercream:
250g unsalted butter (softened)
500g icing sugar
120ml whiskey
Large piping bag fitted with
   large round or star nozzle

m

1. Preheat the oven to 180ºC (160ºC fan).
2. Cream the butter and sugar until light and fluffy.
3. Add the eggs one at a time, beating well in-between each egg to avoid curdling. Beat in one third of the flour, followed by half the Drambuie, and beat until fully incorporated. Repeat, then finish with the remaining flour.
4. Fill the cupcake cases two thirds full and bake in the centre of the oven for 24 minutes, or until a skewer inserted in the middle of a cupcake comes out clean.
5. Once cooked, allow the cakes to cool in the tin for 5 minutes, then remove and continue to cool on a wire rack.

Whiskey buttercream:

1. Beat the butter with an electric whisk until light and fluffy. Sieve the icing sugar into the butter, add the whiskey and fold together using a flat knife.
2. Once most of the icing sugar has been incorporated, finish beating with the whisk to combine fully.

 # RUSTY NAIL

1 BRONZE BEAUTY

Bronze sugar crystals

Pipe a swirl of whiskey buttercream on each
cupcake, then roll the edge of each cupcake in
bronze sugar crystals to create a decorated rim.

RUSTY NAIL

2 NAILED IT!

White candy sticks
Sugarpaste (approx 25g)
Edible glue
Clean pencil sharpener
Bronze edible dust or paint
Bronze edible glitter

First, snap each candy stick two thirds of the way along, then mould a small amount of sugarpaste into a flat disc and attach to the top of the shorter ends with edible glue. Sharpen one end of the longer sticks with a spotlessly clean pencil sharpener. Paint all the candy sticks with bronze edible dust mixed with water, or with bronze edible paint and while still damp, sprinkle with bronze edible glitter.

Pipe a swirl of whiskey buttercream onto each cupcake using a large star nozzle, then lay the "nail" either side of the peaked swirl so that it appears to be nailed right through. Finish with a little extra glitter around the nail for rust.

RUSTY NAIL

3 R.I.P

Grey sugarpaste (approx 200g)
coffin template (see p165)
Black edible pen
Bronze sugar crystals
Green paste food colouring

Roll out the grey sugarpaste and use the template to cut
24 coffin shapes. On 12 of these, write 'R.I.P' with the edible
pen, and push bronze sugar crystals around the edges for
nails. Remove the centres from the remaining 12, using a
sharp knife. Leave to harden for an hour or so.

Colour the whiskey buttercream green then pipe a swirl onto
each cupcake using a large round nozzle. Lay the hollowed
coffin on top of the cupcake first, and the decorated coffin
on top of that, at an angle, as though the occupant has just
escaped...

BLOODY MARY

LIVEN UP YOUR HALLOWEEN PARTY WITH THESE DEVILISHLY SPICY LITTLE MORSELS. ADD A FEW EXTRA SPLASHES OF TABASCO AND THEY BECOME MORE OF A TRICK THAN A TREAT!

preparation time:
25 minutes

cooking time:
22-24minutes

Makes 12 cupcakes

i

Cupcakes:
115g unsalted butter (softened)
270g caster sugar
3 medium eggs
225g self raising flour
1 tsp ground cinnamon
¼ tsp ground nutmeg
75ml tomato juice   }
75ml vodka   } mixed
Dash of tabasco –   }
    to taste
Red paste food colouring

...and to drizzle:
45ml vodka   }
45ml tomato juice   } mixed
Dash of tabasco –   }
    to taste

Vodka glace icing:
500g icing sugar, sieved
85-90ml vodka
Red paste food colouring

m

1. Preheat the oven to 180°C (160°C fan).
2. Cream the butter and sugar until light and fluffy.
3. Add the eggs one at a time, beating well
    in-between each egg to avoid curdling.
    Sift together the flour, cinnamon and nutmeg,
    then beat in one third of this mixture followed
    by half the vodka mixture, and beat until fully
    incorporated. Repeat, finishing with the
    remaining flour mixture.
4. Fill the cupcake cases half full and bake in the
    centre of the oven for 22-24 minutes, or until a
    skewer inserted in the middle of a cupcake comes
    out clean.
5. Once cooked, allow the cakes to cool in the tin for
    5 minutes, then remove and continue to cool on a
    wire rack.
6. Once cooled, trim off the centre of the cupcakes if
    they've peaked, and make holes in the top using a
    skewer. Drizzle generously with the vodka/tomato
    mix.

Vodka glace icing:
Mix the icing sugar with the vodka and red food
colouring until it is bright red and the consistency of
thick double cream. Add more vodka or icing sugar
as necessary. If not using immediately, cover the
icing tightly with cling film to prevent crusting.

BLOODY MARY

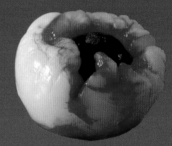

1 AN EYE FOR AN EYE

1 tin lychees in syrup
Strawberry syrup (you can add a touch of red
   paste food colouring for extra gore)
Fresh blueberries

Spoon vodka glace icing over the cupcake, up to the level of
the rim of the case and allow to set. Drain the lychees and pat
dry, then drop a spoonful of strawberry syrup into the middle
of each lychee. Place a blueberry on top, pushing it in slightly
so that the strawberry oozes out of the "eyeball". Spooky!!

BLOODY MARY

2 DRUNKEN CELERY

Celery sticks cut into lengths of approx 8cm.
Chilled vodka (the colder the better)
Cocktail sticks

Make several lengthways slits through the top half of the celery sticks. Pour the chilled vodka into a bowl and lay the celery in the alcohol, ensuring it is well submerged. Refrigerate for an hour or so until the celery starts to fan out. Pat dry then push a cocktail stick halfway into the bottom of the celery, to help fix the celery into the cake.

Spoon the vodka glace icing on top of the cupcake and immediately push in the celery stick, before the icing starts to set, otherwise you will find the icing cracks.

Vodka infused celery is best used immediately otherwise the celery starts to go limp. If you prefer to make these well in advance, you'll have to forgo the vodka and use iced water instead. This version holds its crunch and colour much longer.

BLOODY MARY

3 OFF WITH HER HEAD!

Sugarpaste (approx 260g)
Peach food colouring
Red and black edible pens

Chocolate sticks
Edible silver dust or paint

Spoon vodka glace icing over the cupcake, up to the level of the rim of the case and allow to set.

For the heads, colour approximately 240g of sugarpaste peach and use this to make 12 balls, pulling out a small amount from each for the neck. Snip the bottom of each neck randomly with a pair of scissors to make them look freshly chopped and make small nicks in the top of each head for hair. Poke two small holes for the eyes and a larger one for the astonished mouth. Fill in the eye holes with black edible pen and the mouth with red edible pen. Use the same pen to draw blood on the neck and face.

To make the axe, mould a very small amount of white sugarpaste into the shape of an axe head. Paint with edible silver dust mixed with water or vodka, or with edible silver paint. Break the chocolate sticks in half for the axe handles. Melt a small amount of leftover chocolate and use as glue to stick the handles and axe heads together.

Decorate each cupcake with a head and axe.

IRISH COFFEE

THIS COMBINATION OF RICH IRISH WHISKEY, AROMATIC COFFEE AND A SMOOTH CREAMY TOPPING IS A PERFECT FINALE TO ANY WINTER CELEBRATION. AND, WITH AN EXTRA SPECIAL CHOCOLATEY SURPRISE INSIDE, YOU HAVE COCKTAIL, DESSERT, COFFEE AND PETIT FOUR... ALL ROLLED INTO ONE!

preparation time:
35 minutes excluding cooling time

cooking time:
24 minutes

Makes 12 cupcakes

i

Cupcakes:
165g unsalted butter (softened)
165g caster sugar
3 medium eggs
200g self raising flour (sifted)
2 rounded tsp espresso powder
50ml Irish whiskey
3-4 tbsp Kahlua to drizzle

And to fill...:
200ml double cream
200g white chocolate
Apple corer

Whiskey whipped cream:
600ml double cream
90ml Irish whiskey
1 tbsp icing sugar
Large piping bag with large round nozzle

m

1. To make the white chocolate ganache, break the chocolate into a heatproof bowl. Pour the cream into a small saucepan and bring to the boil. Remove from the heat and pour immediately over the chocolate, stirring continuously until melted and glossy. Place in the fridge to set for 30–45 minutes.
2. Preheat the oven to 180ºC (160ºC fan).
3. Dissolve the espresso powder in the whiskey and set aside.
4. Cream the butter and sugar until light and fluffy.
5. Add the eggs one at a time, beating well in-between each egg to avoid curdling. Beat in one third of the flour , followed by half the whiskey mixture, and beat until fully incorporated. Repeat, finishing with the remaining flour.
6. Fill the cupcake cases two thirds full then bake in the centre of the oven for 24 minutes, or until a skewer inserted in the middle of a cupcake comes out clean.
7. Once cooked, allow the cakes to cool in the tin for 5 minutes, then remove and cool completely on a wire rack.
8. Once cooled, make holes in the top of each cupcake with a skewer and drizzle generously with Kahlua.
9. Use an apple corer to remove a section of sponge from the centre of each cupcake, making sure not to go all the way through, otherwise the filling will dribble out when the case is removed. Spoon a teaspoon or two of the white chocolate ganache filling into the hole – deliciously rich and a lovely surprise.

Whiskey whipped cream:
Whisk the cream, whiskey and icing sugar together until soft peaks form. Serve immediately.

IRISH COFFEE

1 LUCKY FOR SOME

Shamrock cutter
Green sugarpaste (approx 50g)

Cut shamrock shapes from the
green sugarpaste. Pipe a swirl
of whiskey whipped cream onto
each cupcake and decorate with
shamrocks.

IRISH COFFEE

2 CHOCOHOLIC'S DREAM

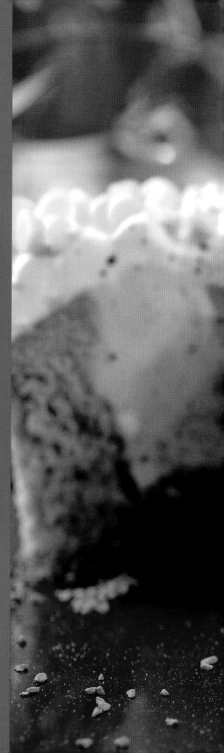

Chocolate beans (or chocolate coffee beans if you prefer)
Mini white chocolate drops

Pipe a swirl of whiskey whipped cream onto each cupcake and edge with chocolate beans. Fill the centre with white chocolate drops – an alcoholic chocoholic's dream cupcake!

IRISH COFFEE

3 ULTIMATE COFFEE

Irish Coffee glass
250g milk or dark chocolate
   (or a mix of the two)
Silicone teaspoon mould (see stockists p157)

Melt the chocolate in a microwave or bain marie and stir until smooth. Pour into the teaspoon moulds and allow to set in the fridge for at least an hour. Remove by gently twisting the mould, and store in the fridge until needed.

Instead of filling the centres of each cupcake with the white chocolate ganache, crumble half a cupcake into an Irish coffee glass, then spoon a generous helping of the ganache on top. Crumble the remaining half cupcake on top of this, and then top with a deep swirl of whiskey whipped cream. Smooth the top with a flat knife and sprinkle with espresso powder. Serve with the chocolate teaspoon for a richly satisfying dessert.

MULLED WINE

THIS IS THE PERFECT TREAT FOR COLD WINTER'S EVENINGS; SPICY AND WARMING, AND YOU CAN STILL DRIVE HOME AFTERWARDS!

preparation time:
35 minutes excluding cooling time

cooking time:
24 minutes

Makes 12 cupcakes

i

Cupcakes:
165g unsalted butter (softened)
165g caster sugar
3 medium eggs
165g self raising flour
1 tsp cinnamon
¼ tsp ground cloves
50ml brandy
Finely grated zest of 1 orange

And to drizzle:
50g orange curd
1 tbsp Grand Marnier
} mixed

Red wine buttercream:
285ml red wine
50g caster sugar
250g unsalted butter (softened)
500g icing sugar
Piping bag with large round or
    star nozzle

1. Preheat the oven to 180°C (160°C fan).
2. Cream the butter and sugar until light and fluffy.
3. Add the eggs one at a time, beating well in-between each egg to avoid curdling. Sift together the flour, cinnamon & cloves. Beat in one third of the flour mixture, followed by half the brandy, and beat until fully incorporated. Repeat, finishing with the remaining flour mixture. Finally, gently fold in the orange zest.
4. Fill the cupcake cases two thirds full then bake in the centre of the oven for 24 minutes, or until a skewer inserted in the middle of a cupcake comes out clean.
5. Once cooked, allow the cakes to cool in the tin for 5 minutes, then remove and cool completely on a wire rack. Once cooled, make holes in the top of each cupcake with a skewer and drizzle generously with the orange curd/Grand Marnier mixture.

Red wine buttercream:

1. Gently heat 225ml of the red wine with the sugar until dissolved, stirring occasionally, then reduce by boiling until syrupy (approx 10 minutes). You should be left with around 80-100ml of liquid. Refrigerate until completely cool (approx 20 minutes).
2. Meanwhile beat the butter with an electric whisk until light and fluffy. Sieve the icing sugar into the butter, and fold together using a flat knife.
3. Once most of the icing sugar has been incorporated, finish beating with the whisk to combine fully.
4. Add the red wine syrup and the remaining red wine and beat well.

139

MULLED WINE

1 CINNAMON CURLS

Biscuit curls

Using a large star nozzle, pipe a swirl of red wine buttercream onto each cupcake and finish with a biscuit curl for a cinnamon stick lookalike.

MULLED WINE

2 SWIRLS & SPRINKLES

Yellow & orange sprinkles

Pipe a swirl of red wine buttercream
onto each cupcake and scatter
liberally with sprinkles.

MULLED WINE

3 PARTY TIME

1 quantity of cinnamon cookie dough
   (see p154)
Square and rectangular cookie cutter (or easily
   cut by hand)
200g sugarpaste in assorted colours
3 tbsp royal icing in 3 assorted colours (see p156)
3 small piping bags fitted with No 2 nozzles

Make the present cookies using the recipe on p154
and the rectangular cutter. Bake for 6-10 minutes
until golden, and allow to cool completely.

Meanwhile, roll out the different coloured
sugarpastes and cut 12 squares and 12 rectangles
the same size as your cookies. Fix the sugarpaste
shapes to the cookies using a barely damp
paintbrush. Pipe lines with the different coloured
royal icings to make the ribbons, and finish with
piped bows.

Pipe a swirl of red wine buttercream on each
cupcake using a star nozzle, and top with one
square and one rectangular cookie.

PEPPERMINT PENGUIN

DON'T PANIC IF YOU'VE FORGOTTEN TO BUY A CHRISTMAS PRESENT FOR THE ONE YOU LOVE – THIS MINTY MOUTHFUL HAS ITS OWN HIDDEN PRESENT INSIDE – A DELICIOUSLY CRUNCHY OREO COOKIE!

preparation time:
25 minutes

cooking time:
24 minutes

Makes 12 cupcakes

i

Cupcakes:
165g unsalted butter (softened)
165g caster sugar
3 medium eggs
135g self raising flour (sifted)
30g cocoa powder (sifted)
50ml crème de menthe liqueur
1 tsp peppermint essence
12 Oreo cookies

Oreo mint buttercream:
250g unsalted butter (softened)
500g icing sugar
100ml mint cream liqueur
(or cream liqueur with 1 tsp peppermint essence added)
3 finely crushed Oreos
Large piping bag with large round or star nozzle

m

1. Preheat the oven to 180ºC (160ºC fan).
2. Cream the butter and sugar until light and fluffy.
3. Add the eggs one at a time, beating well in-between each egg to avoid curdling. Beat in one third of the flour, followed by half the crème de menthe and peppermint essence, and beat until fully incorporated. Repeat, finishing with the remaining flour and the cocoa.
4. Place an Oreo cookie in the base of each cupcake case, then top up the cases with the batter until they are two thirds full. Bake in the centre of the oven for 24 minutes, or until a skewer inserted in the middle of a cupcake comes out clean.
5. Once cooked, allow the cakes to cool in the tin for 5 minutes, then remove and cool completely on a wire rack.

Oreo mint buttercream:

1. Beat the butter with an electric whisk until light and fluffy. Sieve the icing sugar into the butter, and fold together using a flat knife.
2. Once most of the icing sugar has been incorporated, finish beating with the whisk to combine fully.
3. Add the mint cream liqueur a tablespoon at a time, beating well between each addition to avoid curdling. Finally, fold in the crushed Oreo cookies.

PEPPERMINT PENGUIN

1 CRUNCHY SNOWBALLS

Small white sprinkles (non-pareils)

Using a large round nozzle, pipe a mound of Oreo mint buttercream onto each cupcake and smooth into a rounded shape using a flat knife. Pour the sprinkles onto a plate and gently roll the cupcakes in the sprinkles until all the buttercream is covered.

PEPPERMINT PENGUIN

2 CHRISTMAS TREES

Mini Christmas tree sprinkles
Mini red sprinkles

Using a large round nozzle, pipe a swirl
of Oreo mint buttercream onto each
cupcake and decorate with Christmas
trees and balls.

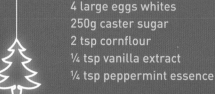

PEPPERMINT PENGUIN

3 PENGUIN PARTY

4 large eggs whites
250g caster sugar
2 tsp cornflour
¼ tsp vanilla extract
¼ tsp peppermint essence

1 tsp white vinegar
2 large piping bags
Large round nozzle
Black edible pen
Blue paste food colour

MERINGUES

1. Preheat the oven to 180ºC (160ºC fan).
2. Beat the egg whites until foamy, then add the sugar (1 tablespoon at a time) and beat until white and glossy. Add the cornflour, vanilla extract, peppermint essence and vinegar and fold in gently to combine.
3. Line a baking tray with non stick baking parchment.
4. Place three quarters of the mixture into a large piping bag fitted with a large round nozzle and the rest into a piping bag without a nozzle, snipping off the tip of the bag after filling. Using the bag with the nozzle, pipe a long sausage (think of it as the bottom of an 'S' shape) pulling it towards you. Then, as though following the line of the 'S', push back approximately a third of the way, and then pull forward again and up, pulling away sharply to give the beak. Use the piping bag without the nozzle to pipe wings either side of the penguin , following the lines of the body.
5. Lower the oven to 155ºC (135ºC fan). Pop the baking tray into the centre of the oven and bake for 25 minutes. Turn off the oven, leaving the meringues to cool inside for a further 25 minutes.
6. When completely cool, dot two eyes with a black edible pen.

Colour the buttercream blue, then use a large round nozzle to pipe a swirl of Oreo mint buttercream onto each cupcake and top with a penguin.

VANILLA COOKIES

preparation time:
20 minutes + 2 hours
chilling time

cooking time: 6-12 minutes

**Makes 1 quantity cookie
dough (12-24 cookies,
depending on size)**

i

200g soft unsalted butter
200g caster sugar
1 medium egg
400g plain flour + extra for
    rolling out
½ tsp vanilla extract

m

1. Preheat the oven to 180°C
   (160°C fan).
2. Line 2 baking trays with baking
   parchment.
3. Cream the butter and sugar
   together using an electric whisk or
   freestanding mixer, until light and
   fluffy (about 2 minutes). Be careful
   not to over beat at this stage, or
   the cookies will spread during
   baking.
4. Beat in the egg and vanilla extract
5. Sift in the flour and beat with a
   wooden spoon until the dough just
   comes together.
6. Tip the dough onto a floured work
   surface and bring together into a
   ball, handling as little as possible
   at this stage.
7. Wrap in plastic wrap and
   refrigerate for an hour.
8. Roll the dough out evenly on a
   floured surface to approximately
   4mm thick. Cut shapes using
   cookie cutters or templates
   (see p164/165) and place them on
   the lined baking trays. Refrigerate
   again for an hour.
9. Bake the cookies for 6-12 minutes
   (depending on size), until lightly
   golden. Allow to cool completely
   before decorating.

CINNAMON COOKIES

Follow Vanilla Cookie recipe, adding 1 tsp ground cinnamon to the flour.

GUINNESS GINGERBREAD COOKIES

preparation time: 20 minutes + 1 hour chilling time

cooking time: 5-8 minutes

Makes 1 quantity cookie dough (12-24 cookies, depending on size)

m

1. Preheat the oven to 180°C (160°C fan).
2. Heat the sugar, golden syrup, butter and Guinness gently until melted.
3. Sift in the flour, bicarbonate of soda, cinnamon and ground ginger and stir to combine.
4. Use your hands to form this into a ball, then wrap in clingfilm and chill for an hour.
5. Remove from the fridge, knead gently, then roll out on a floured surface to around ½ cm thickness. Use cookie cutters or templates (see p164/165) to cut shapes.
6. Place the cookies on a baking tray lined with non-stick paper, then bake for 5-8 minutes until golden.
7. Remove from the oven and transfer to a wire rack after five minutes to cool.

i

60g soft brown sugar
60g golden syrup
35g butter
25ml Guinness
185g plain flour
½ tsp bicarbonate of soda
¼ tsp cinnamon
1 tsp ground ginger

ROYAL ICING

Ready mix royal icing is available from most supermarkets. However if you prefer to make it from scratch, follow this simple recipe.

Makes 1 quantity (approx 280g or 12 tbsp)

i

1 large egg white
250-300g icing sugar (sifted)
juice of up to half a lemon

m

1. Whisk the egg white in a large, clean bowl until foamy. Gradually beat in the icing sugar and continue beating until the icing is bright white and glossy (approximately 2 minutes). Finish beating with a wooden spoon. If needed, add drops of lemon juice sparingly to thin the icing, or a teaspoon of sifted icing sugar to stiffen.
2. Whichever method you choose, transfer the icing immediately to an airtight plastic container, lay some plastic wrap directly on top to prevent crusting, then replace the lid and store in the fridge. It will keep for up to 2 weeks like this if made with very fresh eggs. Before use, bring to room temperature and beat briefly with a wooden spoon.
3. If colouring, gradually add small quantities of paste food colour using a cocktail stick, and mix well.

TOOLS AND EQUIPMENT

To bake the caketails found in this book, you won't need much more than you'll find in any domestic kitchen (and drinks cabinet!). Simple and delicious decoration can be achieved with a sumptuous swirl of icing, needing no more than a piping bag fitted with a large nozzle. Some of the more elaborate decorations may need sugarpaste, paste food colouring, cookie cutters or edible pens – all of which can be found at our stockists listed opposite.

LAKELAND

Order Online:
www.lakeland.co.uk

Order by phone:
Tel: **+44 (01) 5394 88100**
Stores nationwide

SQUIRES

Squires Group
Squires House,
3 Waverley Lane,
Farnham,
Surrey GU9 8BB

Tel: **+44 0845 6171810**

ALMOND ART

Units 15/16
Faraday Close
Gorse Lane Ind Est
Clacton On Sea
Essex CO15 4TR

Tel: **+44 (0) 1255 223322**

**HOPSCOTCH –
ESSENTIAL TREATS**

88 High Street
Barnet, Herts EN5 5SN

Tel: **+44 (020) 8364 9777**
www.hopscotchsweets.co.uk
www.facebook.com/HopscotchTreats

VALENTINE

P.S. I LOVE YOU

1¼ shots Baileys
1¼ shot Amaretto
¾ shot Kahlua
1 shot cream

Mix well and serve in a Martini glass topped with chocolate flakes.

STRAWBERRY DAIQUIRI

2 shots white rum
5 strawberries, or 2 shots strawberry purée
1 shot lime juice
1 tsp sugar

Put all ingredients into a blender together with crushed ice. Blend until smooth. Garnish with a strawberry.

BELLINI

2 shots peach purée
½ shot peach schnapps
top up with champagne

Put the first 2 ingredients into a champagne glass and stir them together. Top up the glass with champagne.

NAUGHTY BUT NICE

BETWEEN THE SHEETS

½ shot rum
½ shot Triple Sec
¼ shot lime juice
½ shot soda

Mix well and serve with flamed orange peel in a Martini glass.

BLUSHING GEISHA

2 shots sake
1 shot pomegranate juice
2 shots rose nectar
1 lime wedge

Pour the ingredients into a mixing glass filled with ice and stir well.

Strain into a stemmed glass or over ice in a Martini glass.

Garnish with a lime wedge.

SEX ON THE BEACH

2 shots vodka
½ shot peach schnapps
½ shot crème de cassis
1½ shot orange juice
2 shots cranberry juice

Mix well and serve in a Hurricane glass.

BLACK TIE

BLACK VELVET

3½ shots Guinness
Champagne

Pour Guinness into glass and top up with champagne.

COSMOPOLITAN

1 shot vodka
1 shot Cointreau
2 shots cranberry juice
½ shot lime juice
dash of grenadine

Pour all the ingredients into a shaker with ice and shake well. Garnish with orange zest, or orange wedge.

MARTINI

3 shots vodka
Dash white vermouth
3 olives

Shake the vodka and vermouth with ice and strain into a chilled Martini glass.

SUMMER

BLUE LAGOON

1 shot vodka
1 shot blue Curaçao
1 shot pineapple juice
Splash of lemonade
Splash of lime juice

Mix well and serve on crushed ice in a long drink glass. Garnish with a lemon slice.

MOJITO

2 shots rum
2 tsp brown sugar
15 mint leaves
lime wedges
soda

Muddle all ingredients together (except soda) until the sugar is dissolved. Pour into glass filled with crushed ice and top up with soda.

PIÑA COLADA

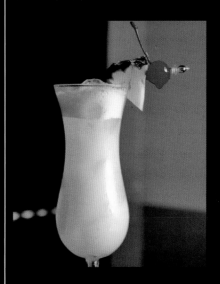

2 shots rum
4 shots pineapple juice
1 shot coconut cream
1 shot double cream

Shake, pour into a Hurricane glass and garnish with pineapple.

ZOMBIE

¾ shot Bacardi
¾ shot spiced rum
¾ shot gold rum
½ shot apricot brandy
2½ shots orange juice
2½ shots pineapple juice
1 shot lime juice
½ shot grenadine

Mix well and serve in
Hurricane glass.

RUSTY NAIL

2 shots whiskey
¾ shot Drambuie

Mix well and serve in a rock
glass on ice.

BLOODY MARY

2½ shots vodka
2 shots tomato juice
¼ shot lemon juice
5 dashes of Worcestershire sauce
4 pinches salt
2 pinches pepper
2 dashes tabasco

Shake all ingredients with ice and
strain into a rock glass. Garnish
with a celery stick.

CHRISTMAS

IRISH COFFEE

1½ shots Irish whiskey
1 cup strong black coffee
Dash Kahlua
whipped cream

Pour ingredients into tall coffee glass and top with whipped cream.

MULLED WINE

Glass red wine
2 slices of orange
1 shot brandy
3 cloves
1 tsp sugar
1 cinnamon stick

Gently heat all ingredients in a saucepan until sugar is dissolved. Serve in an Irish Coffee glass.

PEPPERMINT PENGUIN

3 Oreo cookies
½ shot crème de menthe
½ shot Baileys
3 shots double cream

Combine all ingredients with 1 cup of crushed ice in a blender. Blend until smooth and garnish with a crumbled cookie.

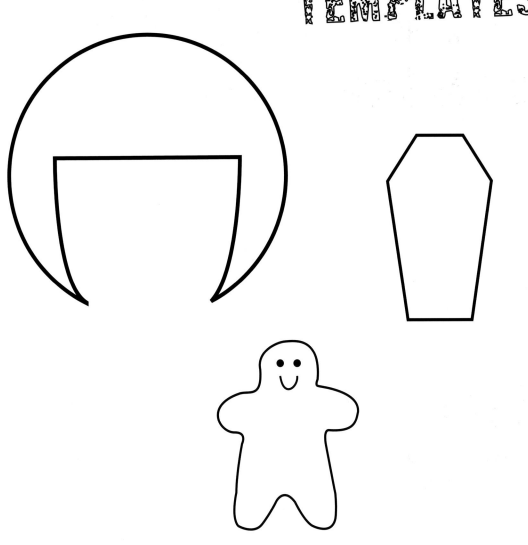

Almond

The Zombies are Coming 110

Amaretto

Creamy Coffee	10
Confetti & Chocolate	12
PS I Love You	8, 158
Rich & Dark	14

Apricot brandy

Bloodbath	108
Dead Easy	112
The Zombies are Coming 110	
Zombie	106, 162

Baileys Irish Cream

Creamy Coffee	10
Confetti & Chocolate	12
PS I Love You	8, 158
Peppermint Penguin	163
Rich & Dark	14

Blueberry

An Eye for an Eye	124

Blue Curaçao

Blue Lagoon	80, 161
Glitzy Cherries	82
Marine Life	86
Vodka Jellies	84

Brandy

Between the Sheets	32, 159
Cinnamon Curls	140
Do Not Disturb!	34
Love in the Afternoon	38
Mulled Wine	138, 163
Party Time	144
Swirls & Sprinkles	142
Unbridled Passion	36

Celery

Drunken Celery	126

Champagne

Bellini	24, 158
Black Gold	58
Black Velvet	56, 160
Caramelised Peaches	28
Chocolate Truffles	60
Dessert a Deux	30
Mine's a Pint	62
Simply Champagne	26

Cherry

Bloodbath	108
Fresh & Fruity	98
Glitzy Cherries	82
Rich & Dark	14

Chocolate

Beach party	102
Chocoholic's Dream	134
Chocolate Mint Leaves	94
Chocolate Truffles	60
Confetti & Chocolate	12
Dead Easy	112
Irish Coffee	130, 163
Lucky for Some	132
Perfect Pineapples	100
Rich & Dark	14
Ultimate Coffee	136

Cinnamon

An Eye for an Eye	124
Bloody Mary	122, 162
Cinnamon Cookie	144, 154
Cinnamon Curls	140
Drunken Celery	126
Mulled Wine	138, 163
Off with her Head	128
Party Time	144
Swirls & Sprinkles	142

Coconut

Beach Party	102
Fresh & Fruity	98
Perfect Pineapples	100
Pina Colada	96, 161

Cointreau

Cosmopolitan	64, 160
Heart to Heart	70
Orange Drizzle	66
Pure Decadence	68

Cranberries

Cosmopolitan	64, 160
Fun in the Sun	54
Gingerbread Lovers	52
Heart to Heart	68
Hello Cheeky	50
Orange Drizzle	66
Pure Decadence	68
Sex on the Beach	48, 159

Crème de Cassis

Fun in the Sun	54
Gingerbread Lovers	52
Hello Cheeky	50
Sex on the Beach	48, 159

Crème de Menthe

Chocolate Mint Leaves	94
Christmas Trees	150
Clearly Minty	92
Crunchy Snowballs	148
Mojito	88,161
Penguin Party	152,
Peppermint Penguin	146 ,163
Pure & Simple	90

Dark Rum

Bloodbath	108
Dead Easy	112
The Zombies are Coming 110	
Zombie	106,162

Drambuie

Bronze Beauty	116
Nailed It!	118
R.I.P	120
Rusty Nail	114,162

Espresso

Chocoholic's Dream	134
Creamy Coffee	10
Confetti & Chocolate	12
Irish Coffee	130, 163
Lucky for Some	32
PS I Love You	8, 158
Rich & Dark	14
Ultimate Coffee	136

Ginger

Guinness Gingerbread Cookies	52, 62, 155

Guinness

Black Gold	58
Black Velvet	56, 160
Chocolate Truffles	60
Guinness Gingerbread Cookies	52, 62, 155
Mine's a Pint	62

Gold Leaf

Pure Decadence	68

Grand Marnier

Cinnamon Curls	140
Mulled Wine	138, 163
Swirls & Sprinkles	142
Party Time	144

Irish Whiskey

Chocoholic's Dream	134
Irish Coffee	130, 163
Lucky for Some	132
Ultimate Coffee	136

Kahlua

Chocoholic's Dream	134
Creamy Coffee	10
Confetti & Chocolate	12
Irish Coffee	130, 163
Lucky for Some	132
PS I Love You	8, 158
Rich & Dark	14
Ultimate Coffee	136

THANKS

WE WOULD LIKE TO DEDICATE THIS BOOK TO ALL OUR LOVELY FRIENDS – WITH WHOM WE'VE SPENT MANY HAPPY HOURS DRINKING COCKTAILS AND EATING CUPCAKES!

Special thanks go to our publisher, Peter Marshall from Chef Media, who not only encouraged us to write this book, but also took the amazing photographs – It was a lucky day when we were placed on neighbouring stands at the Squires Sugarcraft Show in March 2013. Also thanks to Philip Donnelly, for turning the photos and text into the work of art you see before you, and to Celine from Squires, and Kelly from Lakeland for their continuing generosity in supplying the equipment needed to produce this book. Finally, as ever, thanks to Andy, Jeremy, Ashley, Elena, Joe and Jake for always cheering us on from the sidelines.